Books are to be returned on or before
the last date below.

2 5 JUN 201		

LIBREX—

MACMILLAN READERS

ELEMENTARY LEVEL

Founding Editor: John Milne

The Macmillan Readers provide a choice of enjoyable reading materials for learners of English. The series is published at six levels – Starter, Beginner, Elementary, Pre-intermediate, Intermediate and Upper.

Level control
Information, structure and vocabulary are controlled to suit the students' ability at each level.

The number of words at each level:

Starter	about 300 basic words
Beginner	about 600 basic words
Elementary	about 1100 basic words
Pre-intermediate	about 1400 basic words
Intermediate	about 1600 basic words
Upper	about 2200 basic words

Vocabulary
Some difficult words and phrases in this book are important for understanding the story. Some of these words are explained in the story and some are shown in the pictures. From Pre-intermediate level upwards, words are marked with a number like this: ...[3]. These words are explained in the Glossary at the end of the book.

Contents

3

The People in this Story

Victor Frankenstein

Elizabeth

Henry Clerval

The Monster

Victor's father

Victor's brother, William

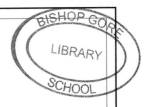
Frankenstein

I am the most unhappy
man in the world. I
have followed the Monster
to this place of ice and
snow. I know he is near.
I must find him. I gave
the Monster life, but now
I must kill him. Then
I will kill myself — I
will die alone in this
terrible place.

1

I Go to University

My name is Frankenstein – Victor Frankenstein. I was born in 1810 in the beautiful city of Geneva, in Switzerland. My father and mother loved me very much and my early life was happy. My younger brother, William, was born when I was twelve years old.

Two years later, my dear Elizabeth came to live with us. She was the daughter of my father's best friend. When Elizabeth's parents died, Elizabeth came to live with us in our house. I loved her from that time.

I was a good pupil at school and always came first in the examinations. I was always interested in science. I wanted to learn about human life. I wanted to learn more in order to help people. I wanted to make their lives better.

When I was eighteen, my mother died. Before she died, my mother spoke to Elizabeth and myself.

'My children,' she said, 'I hope that one day you will marry. Then you, my dear Elizabeth, can look after little William.'

My mother looked at me and smiled.

'My dear Victor, the family hopes that you will do great things,' she said. 'Soon you are going to the University. I know you will work hard. Perhaps, one day, you will be famous. You have been a good son and I can die happy.'

I cried when my mother died. But now I am glad that she is dead. My work has brought death and sadness to the world. Because of me, the people I loved have died.

Three weeks after my mother's death, I left Geneva. I was going to study at the great German University of Heidelburg.

In the morning, I said goodbye to my father, to Elizabeth and to my little brother, William.

I spent my last evening in Geneva with my friend, Henry Clerval.

'You are lucky, Victor,' Henry said. 'I wish I was going with you. But my father wants me to work in the family business. You will become a doctor or professor. Your work will be known all over the world.'

'We shall always be friends, Henry,' I told him. 'I shall see you soon. We shall be together again in the holidays.'

'Write to me soon, Victor,' Henry said.

'Of course,' I answered.

In the morning, I said goodbye to my father, to Elizabeth

and to my little brother, William. I was sorry to leave home. But I wanted to go to University. I wanted to study and to learn everything.

How I wished that I had never left Geneva!

2

The Secret of Life

I was very happy at the University. I worked hard and my professors were very pleased with me. I studied science – chemistry and medicine. I wanted to learn everything about the human body. I also wanted to learn about the mind of man.

Most of all I wanted to learn the secret of life. What was the difference between a living person and a dead body? Why did a dead body turn to dust? Could a dead man come alive again?

I worked hard to find the answers to these questions. I read many old books. The writers said it was possible to create life. They said it was possible to make a dead man live again. But the writers did not say how it could be done.

I lived in a house in the old part of the city. I had a laboratory there where I worked alone. No one knew what I was doing.

In the evenings, I read in my library. Sometimes I did not sleep all night. The months passed and I forgot about my family and my friends. I had only one thought. I wanted to find the secret of life.

I went to hospitals and watched men dying. I listened to their cries. I watched their bodies grow old and ugly.

I paid men to steal bodies from graveyards. These men dug up the bodies from the ground. They brought them to my laboratory at night. I cut up the bodies. Everywhere I smelt death – death and blood.

People were frightened of me, but I did not care. I knew that death would change them. Their blood would stop

I paid men to steal bodies from graveyards.

moving. Their skin would become wrinkled and yellow. I wanted to help them. I was working hard to find the secret of life.

I bought blood from living men. Was the secret of life in the blood? I looked at men's brains, soft and grey. Was the secret of life there?

Then, one night, there was a terrible storm. The sky was covered with black clouds. Thunder crashed and the rain fell. Lightning flashed in the sky. Suddenly the lightning gave me an idea. I knew what I had to do.

I began my work carefully. I took parts of dead men from hospitals and graveyards. I put the parts together to make a human body. I was making a man – a huge man – the biggest, strongest man who had ever lived. This man was going to come alive. I had found a way to create life. This man was going to live.

He was a good-looking man. His face was handsome and kind. His huge body was strong and well-made.

Day by day, I joined each part together. At last he was ready. He was ready to receive life. The body lay on a table in my laboratory. I had joined the hands, feet and head to metal wires. These wires went up to the roof of my house. Now I had to wait for a storm. When the power of the lightning flashed down through the wires, the man would live!

A few days later clouds covered the sun. The sky became dark. I knew a storm was coming. I opened the windows of the laboratory and waited.

Lightning began to flash and I heard thunder. A flash again and now the thunder was nearer. Then the lightning was all around me. It flashed blue and silver. Thunder crashed and the room was as light as day.

Suddenly it happened. The lightning hit the wires on the roof. The sparks of light came down the wires. I looked at the huge body. The silver light reached the hands, the feet and the head. The body was covered with a blue and silver light. For a moment everything was quiet. Was it moving? No, yes! An arm moved and then a leg. Then I heard breathing, yes, the man was breathing. He was alive!

The body moved and I went nearer. I held out my arms and smiled. The man sat up and turned his head. His eyes were open.

Oh, God. What had I done? What had gone wrong?

The man's skin was wrinkled and yellow. His eyes were yellow and dry. His thin, black lips opened in a terrible smile. I had not made a man. I had made a Monster!

I ran out of my laboratory and down the stairs. I heard the slow, heavy footsteps of the Monster as he followed me.

There was another flash of lightning. Thunder crashed over the house. I stopped and looked back. The Monster was standing at the top of the stairs. Behind him were red and yellow flames. Fire! My laboratory was on fire!

I gave a terrible cry as the Monster moved towards me. Then I fell down and everything went black.

The man sat up and turned his head. His eyes were open.

The First Death

When I woke up, I was in a strange bed, in a strange room. I looked round in surprise. Where was I? What had happened? I turned my head. Someone was sitting beside the bed. It was my dear friend, Henry Clerval.

'My dear Henry,' I cried, 'How glad I am to see you. But why are you here? What has happened?'

'Thank God you are alive, Victor,' Henry said. 'Your house was struck by lightning last night. A fire started and the house was burnt to the ground. All your books and papers were destroyed. There is nothing left of your laboratory.'

I smiled. 'I don't care, Henry,' I said. 'I was tired of my work. My ideas were wrong. But tell me, Henry, what are you doing in Heidelburg?'

'Your father sent me,' Henry said. 'When you did not write, he became worried. What is wrong, Victor? You look very pale and ill.'

'Nothing is wrong now,' I said. 'I was working too hard. But that is finished now. I don't want to talk about it any more, Henry. Tell me the news from Geneva.'

'Everyone is well,' Henry answered. 'Your family send you their love. And I am coming to the University to study. My father has agreed at last. I am going to study languages.'

I was very happy that Henry had come to Heidelburg. The past years seemed like a dream. Thank God! The fire had destroyed the terrible Monster. I knew now that my work had been very wicked. I hated science now. I decided to study languages with Henry.

Someone was sitting beside the bed. It was my dear friend,
Henry Clerval.

The months passed. Slowly I became stronger and happier. I was a young man. I made friends and began to enjoy life again.

Winter passed and Spring. Then in May, a letter came from my father.

As I began to read it, I gave a terrible cry.

'My God, Victor, what's wrong?' Henry asked. 'Is it bad news?'

dramatic 'Terrible news,' I answered. 'My brother, William, is dead.'

'Dead?' Henry repeated. 'Has there been an accident?'

'Not an accident,' I answered. 'My dear brother, only ten years old, has been killed – murdered! I must go home at once.'

I got ready for my journey like a man in a dream. I said goodbye to Henry and left Heidelburg – for the last time. The long journey went quickly. Soon I was looking at the villages and mountains near Geneva. I had not seen my home for nearly four years.

In the afternoon of the twentieth day, I arrived at a small village about half a kilometre from Geneva. It was the place where my brother had been murdered. I decided to stay the night in the village. I wanted to see the place where William had died.

It was a beautiful place. I stood there thinking about my brother. Why had anyone wanted to kill him? I could not understand it. It was nearly dark now. I heard thunder. Lightning began to flash in the mountains.

Something moved behind a tree. There was another flash of lightning. For a moment I saw everything clearly. There was something huge and terrible there! Something bigger than any man. It was the Monster. There was a wicked

20

smile on his yellow, wrinkled face.

I suddenly understood. The Monster was not dead. He had not died in the fire. And now the Monster had killed *ironic* my brother. I gave a cry. The Monster turned away. I ran after him, but he was moving too fast.

A few minutes later, I saw him climbing up the side of the mountain. The Monster was faster and stronger than any man. I knew that I could not catch him.

I had made a Monster. And the Monster had murdered my brother. How could I tell my father? I could not tell him the truth. He would not believe me.

My mind was full of terror and fear. But I could not tell anyone my terrible secret. I went on to Geneva with a sad heart.

*A few minutes later, I saw him climbing up the side of the
mountain.*

Home Again

I was home again at last. But how unhappy I was! My father looked like an old man. My dear Elizabeth's face was thin and sad.

Elizabeth showed me a picture of my mother. It was a small painting in a gold frame.

'Look, Victor,' Elizabeth said. 'William died because of this picture. He was wearing it on a gold chain on the day he died. He wore the picture round his neck. The picture is very valuable. That is why the murderer took it. William was killed for this picture.'

'Then you know who the murderer is?' I cried. 'You have seen him!'

'Him?' my father repeated in surprise. 'No, Victor, the murderer is a woman. She is the young girl who looked after William. We thought she was a good girl, but she killed our dear boy.'

'What do you mean?' I asked him. 'I know the murderer. I have seen him.'

'How can you know the murderer?' Elizabeth asked me. 'You have just come back to Geneva, Victor. No, this picture was found in the young girl's hand. She is guilty. We know she killed William. She is in prison now.'

'She is not guilty,' I cried. 'I must talk to someone. I must tell what I know. I must go to the prison at once.'

'You are too late,' my father said. 'She is going to die. She will be hanged at ten o'clock this morning.'

'I must see her,' I cried. 'I know the truth. Someone must listen to me.'

dramatic

23

I was home again at last.

I took a horse and rode as fast as I could to the prison. There were many people standing outside the prison gates.

I jumped down from my horse. At that moment, the clock struck ten. The crowd of people shouted, 'She's dead. She's dead.'

I turned away and my eyes were full of tears. Two innocent people had died – first my brother and now this young girl. They had died because of me. I was a murderer too.

I returned to the house sadly. But I did not want to stay with my father and Elizabeth. I was afraid to tell them the truth. I knew the Monster had murdered William. And I had made the Monster. I could not live at home with my terrible secret.

I decided to go away alone. Perhaps I could forget everything in the beautiful mountains of Switzerland. I packed my bags and went into the mountains. It was the middle of summer but the weather was bad. In the high mountains, the wind blew strongly. The rain fell and the air was cold. But I did not care. I went up, higher and higher.

I came to the highest mountain and I went on climbing. The path was very steep, but I walked slowly on. It was midday when I reached the top. The sun shone on the ice and snow. For the first time since William's death, I began to feel happy.

As I rested there, I saw a figure coming towards me. It was walking quickly over the ice. Was it a man? It was moving too quickly. The figure came nearer and nearer. As I looked, a feeling of terror came into my heart. I stood up. It was the Monster!

'Stop!' I cried. 'Don't come near me! Why are you living when my brother is dead? I must destroy you before you murder again.'

'You made me,' the Monster answered. 'If I kill, you are
guilty. But do not hate me. I do not want to kill. If you help
me, I can live happily.'

'Why should I help you?' I cried.

'Because you made me,' the Monster repeated. 'And
remember, I am bigger and stronger than you. I can kill you
easily. No one will find you here.'

I was not afraid. I was going to kill the Monster. But as I
moved towards the Monster, he spoke again.

'Stop,' he said. 'You must listen to my story. When you
gave me life, I was not wicked. But you made me ugly.
Because of that, all living things hate me. So I hate you, my
maker.'

'Tell me your story quickly,' I answered.

5

The Monster's Story

'I remember the heat of the fire,' the Monster said. 'I remember running away from it. I ran and ran through the city. It was dark and no one saw me. I did not know who I was. I did not know where I was going. Many days passed.'

'How did you live?' I asked him. 'What did you eat?'

'Sometimes I ate fruit from the trees,' the Monster answered. 'Sometimes I took food from houses. The first time I did this, a man saw me. I shall never forget the fear in his eyes. I could not understand it. I wanted to be friends with him. I smiled at him, but he ran away. *Sympothy for the monster*

'A few days later, I came to a small pool of water. When I bent down to drink, I saw my own face. How horrible it was! How different from other people's faces! I saw my yellow, wrinkled skin. I saw my yellow eyes and thin, black lips. Now I knew why people ran away from me. From that moment, I hated myself. And I hated you, Victor Frankenstein.' *empathy*

'How do you know my name?' I cried.

'The laboratory was on fire,' the Monster replied. 'I picked up your cloak to protect myself from the fire. I used it to cover myself. Later, I found a book in the pocket with your name in it. I made a promise to myself. Everyone with that name was my enemy. Everyone with that name would die. I would wander through the world looking for my revenge.

'I walked on for many days,' the Monster continued. 'At last, I came to a beautiful valley. At the end of the valley, there was a little cottage. I hid myself and watched the cottage. Three people lived there – an old man, a young man and a girl.

'They were poor, but very happy. Why? Because they loved each other. I watched them for several days.

'The old man never moved from the cottage. The young people worked hard all day. Then they came back with food or wood.

'In the evenings, they all sat together. I watched them through a small hole in the wall. The house was full of books. The old man was blind. He could not see. The young girl read aloud from the books to the old man. I listened too. I learnt many, many things.

'One day, I watched the young people go out. I knew they would be away all day. I knocked at the cottage door. The old man answered and I went in. I knew that he could not see me.

' "I am a stranger in this country," I said. "A terrible accident has made my face ugly. People are afraid of me. But I must talk to someone. Can I talk to you?"

'The old man smiled and told me to sit down. I began to talk and we soon became friends. The old man was very clever.

'He became my teacher,' the Monster said. 'His cottage was my school. I wanted to be part of his family. But I always left the cottage before the young people returned.

'Then, one day, I stayed late. The young girl came into the cottage and saw me. She screamed loudly and I ran to the door of the cottage. The girl was terrified and fell to the ground. I bent over to help her. At that moment, her brother came running up. He saw me and shot at me with his gun. I cried out in pain and ran away down the valley.

'My mind was full of anger. I hated everyone in the world

– men, women and children. But most of all, I hated you, Victor Frankenstein. You made me ugly. You made me a Monster who everyone fears.'

The unhappy Monster looked around him.

'And so my wanderings began again,' he went on. 'I came at last to these mountains. But their beauty did not please me. I went on until I was near the city of Geneva. I was lonely and tired. Would I ever find a friend?

'One day, I saw a little child. He was running about happily and singing to himself. There was no one near us. I had an idea. I would make this child my friend. He would not fear me. We would live happily together.

'I stood up quietly and took the child by the arm. But when he saw my face, he screamed and screamed. "Let me go," he cried. "Let me go. I will tell my father."

' "No, you must come with me!"

' "But my father is an important man. His name is Frankenstein. He will put you in prison if you hurt me."

'Frankenstein! It was the name of my enemy. I put my hands round the child's neck. Soon he stopped moving. He was dead and I had killed him.

'Then I saw the picture round his neck. I took it from his neck and held it in my hand. The woman in the picture was smiling. But no woman would ever smile at me. I hurried away from the dead child. I saw a young woman asleep under a tree. I put the picture in her hand. People would think she had killed the child. She would die, too.

'That is my story, Victor Frankenstein,' the Monster said. 'What can you say to me now?'

I saw a young woman asleep under a tree.

6

The Monster's Request

'What can I say?' I repeated. 'My wickedness has brought terror and unhappiness to the world. I made you. Now I must find the strength to kill you.'

The Monster smiled. It was a terrible smile.

'You do not have the strength to kill me,' he said. 'And I do not want to kill you. No. You must live. You must do something for me.'

'For you? Never!' I cried.

'You must,' the Monster said. 'Listen to me. No man or woman will ever be my friend. You must create a friend for me. You must create a woman who can love me. She must be ugly and terrible, like me.'

'I will never make another Monster,' I said. 'You have brought enough unhappiness to the world.'

'I have brought unhappiness because I am unhappy,' the Monster replied. 'Now only you can help me. Only you can make my life happy.'

I thought for a moment.

'If I do it, then you must go far away,' I said. 'You and your woman must live far from towns and people. You must live in a lonely place where there are no other people.'

The Monster was silent for a few moments. Then he spoke.

'I agree,' the Monster said. 'Give me what I ask. Then you will never see me again. Begin your work at once. I shall return when the woman is ready. Until then, goodbye.'

And without another word, the Monster left me alone on the mountain.

What could I do? I did not want to make another Monster. I thought again of the blood and of the horror. Could I work with dead bodies again? Could I live again with the smell of death and blood?

I knew the Monster would come back. I had to do what he asked. If I did not, he would kill me. I did not care about that. But perhaps he would destroy my family. Perhaps he would kill my dear Elizabeth.

I did not know what to do. I decided to go back to Geneva. First of all, I had to see my family again.

I had been away from Geneva for nearly two months. My father was very happy to see me.

'You still look ill, Victor,' he said. 'Your holiday has not done you any good. You need company. It is not right for you to be always alone.'

'Yes, father. We all need someone to love,' I said sadly. I was thinking of the Monster. Like everyone else, he wanted someone to love.

'I have an important question to ask you, Victor,' my father went on.

'What is it, father?' I said.

'Do you love Elizabeth?' my father asked.

'Of course I do,' I answered. 'I loved her from the first time I saw her.'

'But do you love her as a sister – or as a wife?'

I thought of my unhappy life. I thought of Elizabeth's beauty. I did not have to live alone. I could be happy. Then I remembered the Monster. I was afraid of him. I had to do what he asked.

I waited for a few minutes before I spoke. Then I looked at my father.

'I love Elizabeth and I want to make her my wife,' I said

33

slowly. 'But not yet. I still have work to do. I must leave Geneva and work alone.'

'What is this work?' my father asked. 'You work too hard, Victor. You will be ill again. Why don't you stay here with your friends?'

Yes, I did want to stay in Geneva! But I knew that the Monster would be watching me.

'No, father, I must go,' I said.

Before I left, I spoke to my dear Elizabeth alone.

'Wait for me, Elizabeth,' I said. 'I shall be back when my work is finished. Wait for me, my dear love. When I come back, we shall be married.'

'I shall wait for you for ever, Victor,' Elizabeth answered.

'God bless you,' I said. 'Give me a few more months. It is all I need.'

I prepared myself for a long journey. I had to find somewhere to live. I had to find somewhere far away from Geneva. I had to find somewhere where I could make the female Monster. But where could I go? Where could I do my wicked work in secret?

The answer to these questions came in a letter. It was a letter from Henry Clerval in Strasbourg.

My dear Victor, (Henry wrote)
I have a job here. I am teaching languages at the University. Why don't you come and visit me? Strasbourg is a beautiful city. I have not seen you for a long time. We have many things to talk about. Also a holiday will do you good. Let me know when you are coming.
Your friend, Henry.

I wrote to Henry. I agreed to visit him.

I knew what I was going to do. After a week or two, I would find a lonely house. I would build a laboratory there. I would work as before, but more quickly. Soon I would be free of the Monster for ever.

7

I Begin My Work

After a few days, I was in the beautiful city of Strasbourg. Henry knew the city well. He showed me the beautiful old buildings. We were happy together.

I found a house outside the city and began my terrible work. Henry was busy at the University. I was able to start quickly. But how I hated my work! This time I knew what I was making. I knew I was making a Monster, not a beautiful woman.

The smell of blood and death made me feel ill. I hated talking to the men who brought me dead bodies. They were wicked men. I knew my work was wicked too. But I went on. I had to. Once more, I began to put the parts of bodies together.

Of course, I did not tell Henry what I was doing. But then he found out everything. It was because of my carelessness.

The Female Monster was almost complete. In a day or two, I would give her the spark of life. I had not seen the Monster. But I knew he was near. He was waiting for me to finish my terrible work.

One night, I was working late. I was very tired. Suddenly, there was a sound outside the room. I turned in fear.

'Go away,' I cried. 'It is not finished yet. You can't come in. It will be ready in two or three days.'

'This is your friend, Henry,' a voice said. 'I've come to see you. Why can't I come in? What's the matter?'

To my horror, the door opened and Henry came into the room. I had forgotten to lock the door!

'Why, Victor, what are you doing?' Henry cried. He looked around the room. 'I did not know you had a laboratory here. What a terrible smell. There is blood everywhere. Why . . . Oh, my God! What is that smell?'

'Don't look, don't look, Henry,' I cried. 'No one must know. No one must know.'

But Henry was already staring at the Female Monster.

'What is this terrible thing?' he whispered. 'Is it a woman? Is she dead or alive? Have you killed her, Victor? Are you mad?'

36

But Henry was already staring at the Female Monster.

At first, I could not speak. I put my face in my hands and began to cry.

'Henry, you have found out my terrible secret. I have to do it. If I don't do it, the Monster will kill again.'

'Monster? What Monster?' Henry asked. 'You are ill, Victor. You must be ill.'

'Perhaps I am,' I replied. 'I must tell you everything.'

Henry listened to my story in horror and amazement. When I had finished, he looked at the Female Monster. Then he spoke.

'Victor,' he said. 'You cannot give this creature life. She may be more wicked than the first Monster. What if they have children? One day these terrible creatures may rule the world. No. It must not happen. You must destroy this creature, Victor. I will help you.'

'No, Henry,' I cried. 'The Monster is near. I know it. He will have his revenge. He will kill you.'

'I don't care,' Henry answered. 'This creature must not live. Help me, Victor. Let us destroy this terrible thing.'

Henry ran to the table and began to pull the wires from the body. Then he began to pull the body apart. I was almost mad with terror. Then I picked up a knife and began to help him.

There was a cry of pain and rage. The Monster was outside the window. He smashed it open and jumped down into the room.

'No, no, you must not destroy her!' the Monster cried. 'She is mine, she is mine.'

The Monster rushed at me. His dry, yellow eyes were full of anger. As his hands reached out, Henry stepped in front of me. The Monster, blind with anger, took hold of Henry's neck. The terrible hands held Henry until he fell dead.

The Monster, blind with anger, took hold of Henry's neck.

'What have you done?' I cried. 'He was my dearest friend. Why do you let me live? Kill me too!'

'No, I'll not kill you. Not yet,' the Monster replied. 'If I kill you, your unhappiness will be at an end. You have destroyed my bride. I will return on your wedding-night, Victor Frankenstein. I will have my revenge.'

The Monster stood silently for a moment. He looked at the blood. He looked at the body that would never live. He looked at the dead body of Henry Clerval. Then he looked at me.

'They are dead, but you will live. You will live until I want to kill you,' the Monster said.

He kicked over the lamps that lit the room. Red and yellow flames began to rise. The laboratory was on fire.

'Good,' the Monster said. 'Soon nothing will be left. But, by then, we shall both be far away.'

I felt his strong arms around me. His body had the smell of death. His skin was hard and dry. With one jump, he was out of the window.

The Monster held me tightly in his arms. He moved with great speed. I could not see. I could not breathe. I knew nothing more.

The Monster held me tightly in his arms. He moved with great speed.

8

My Wedding-night

I opened my eyes and looked around me. I was in a small, white bedroom. The window was small and it had metal bars across it. Where was I?

I tried to sit up, but I could not.

I screamed loudly and at once two men rushed into the room.

'Help me,' I cried. 'Let me go. My name is Victor Frankenstein. Send a message to my father in Geneva. Tell him to come here.'

'Your father is here, Victor,' a quiet voice answered. My father came up to my bed and sat down beside me. How old and grey he looked!

'Oh, father, help me,' I said. 'Take me home.'

My father turned to the two men. 'Bring the doctor,' he said. 'I think my son is well now.'

When the doctor had examined me, he told the men to free me.

'You have been very ill, Doctor Frankenstein,' he said. 'Something terrible has happened to you. You screamed and cried. You said that you were a murderer. You said that you were the murderer of your brother, William, and of your friend, Henry Clerval.'

Henry Clerval! Suddenly my mind was clear again. I remembered everything.

'Henry is dead. Henry is dead,' I cried.

'Yes,' my father answered sadly. 'His body was found in a burning house. But you were many miles away. You did not kill him. And when your brother was killed, you were in Heidelburg.'

'But they died because of me,' I answered.

'That is not true,' my father said. 'You have been ill. But you are better now. I am taking you back to Geneva. Elizabeth is waiting there for you.'

I cannot remember the journey back to my home. I was still very weak. I slept for most of the time.

When I saw my home again, I felt stronger. When I saw my dear Elizabeth's face, I felt happier.

'Elizabeth, my dear Elizabeth,' I said. 'Now I am home with you, I feel well again.'

But I was still afraid. The Monster had killed my friend. He was going to return on my wedding-night. He was going to have his revenge. But now I was prepared. I carried a gun with me always. If I saw the Monster, I would shoot him. I would kill him. The months of fear and terror would be over.

I saw that Elizabeth looked pale and unhappy. I asked her what was wrong.

'Your mother hoped that we would marry. Your father wants us to marry,' she said. 'My feelings for you have not changed. I love you.

'But you have travelled to many places, Victor. You have lived in great cities. Perhaps you love another woman. If you do, please tell me.'

'I do not know a woman as beautiful as you,' I replied. 'I now love you more than ever, Elizabeth. But terrible things have happened to me. The terror is not yet over. My life is in danger. Can you marry a man who may soon die?'

'No one knows when they will die,' Elizabeth answered. 'If you love me, Victor, I will marry you. I will make you happy.'

So we decided on the day of our marriage. When the

After we were married, we left for our honeymoon. The journey started by boat.

Monster came to kill me, I would shoot him. Then I would tell Elizabeth my terrible secret. Her love would save me and protect me.

On our wedding-day, the sun was shining. All the world seemed happy. Elizabeth looked very beautiful.

After we were married, we left for our honeymoon. The journey started by boat. The sun was shining on the water of the lake and on the mountains. I heard the happy cries of our friends as they waved goodbye to us.

Those were the last happy hours that I ever spent. It was getting dark when the boat arrived at a small inn. The inn was beside the lake. The water and the mountains looked very beautiful.

We stayed in the inn that night. After dinner, we went to our room. I was sure that the Monster was near. But I was going to fight for my life and happiness. I had my gun with me.

Elizabeth saw that I was afraid.

'Why are you so afraid, Victor?' she asked. 'Why are you carrying a gun? Who can harm us in this beautiful place?'

'This is a night of great danger,' I replied, 'very great danger. But after this night, we will be happy together.'

I told Elizabeth to stay in the room. I told her to lock the door until I came back. Then I looked through the inn. I went into every room. But the Monster was not there. Perhaps nothing would happen.

Suddenly I heard a terrible scream – and then another. It came from our room. Elizabeth was alone in the room. Then I understood. The Monster was going to kill Elizabeth, not me. This was his revenge.

I called some servants. Together we rushed to the room. We broke down the door.

It was too late. Elizabeth lay dead on our marriage bed.

It was too late. Elizabeth lay dead on our marriage bed.

Her face had a look of terror. Her beautiful hair hung over her lifeless body. The marks of the Monster's hands were on her white neck. The Monster's hard, wrinkled fingers had torn her body. Her white dress was red with blood.

I ran to the window and looked out. In the moonlight, I saw the terrible shape of the Monster. I fired my gun, but the Monster was moving too quickly. In a moment, he had disappeared behind some trees.

People rushed into the room. I do not remember what I said or did. I was taken back to Geneva. I was mad with pain and sadness. When my father heard the news, he became ill. A few weeks later, he died.

For a long time, I lived alone. I saw no one. Perhaps I was mad. I do not know. One day, I went to the graveyard. All the people I loved were there. I looked at William's grave. I looked at Elizabeth's grave. And I looked at the grave of my father and mother.

I stood there and I raised my eyes to the sky. I spoke aloud to God in Heaven.

'I, Victor Frankenstein, doctor of Geneva, say these words. I will spend the rest of my life looking for the Monster. Then I will kill him. I, Victor Frankenstein, created the Monster. I will kill him.'

I stood there looking at the dark clouds above me. Like an answer, I heard a loud terrible laugh. The sound made my blood cold. Then I heard the Monster's voice.

'Now I am happy,' the Monster said. 'I have had my revenge. The rest of your life will be as miserable as mine. Follow me and find me if you can.'

Revenge at Last

Years passed. Now I feel that my life is nearly over.

I followed the Monster wherever he led me. I followed him through forests and across deserts. I crossed flat plains and high mountains.

At last we have reached this place of ice and snow. The cold is terrible. But the Monster feels nothing. He does not feel cold or heat. Always, he has been in front of me. I get near him, but I can never catch him.

Now the journey has ended. The Monster is ready to stand and fight. He is bigger and stronger than me. But I have my gun. I will be able to kill him before he kills me.

I can see the Monster in front of me. His terrible shape looks black against the white snow. He has stopped at last. He has turned to look at me.

'Do not kill me yet, Victor Frankenstein,' the Monster cried. 'Listen to what I have to say.'

'What can you say to me?' I replied. 'You have destroyed everything I loved. You are a thing of evil – a wicked creature.'

'You made me,' the Monster replied. 'You are guilty. I did not wish to be evil. I wanted to be your friend. But you made me ugly. You ran away from me. Those I tried to love were afraid of me. So, I killed them.

'I asked you to create a friend for me. But you destroyed her. I had no family to love, so I destroyed yours.

'My wicked life made me unhappy. But I could not stop. Pain and unhappiness turned to anger in my mind. You are guilty, Frankenstein. You gave me this ugly body. You created me, you are a wicked man.'

As I listened to the Monster's words, my mind was filled with horror.

'What you say is true,' I cried. 'I was the murderer of those I loved!'

'Now you have said these words my life of misery and unhappiness is complete,' said the Monster sadly. 'You are the guilty one, not me. Now I shall go far away from here. I shall find wood. I shall set light to it. Then I shall throw myself on the flames. My death will be terrible. But at last I will be at peace.'

And with one last look at me, the Monster turned and went to his lonely and terrible death.

I have decided to die in this terrible place. The story of my life has ended. Perhaps no one will ever read these words. It does not matter. Here I will stay until my body is hard and cold.

Goodbye — and may God forgive me. These are the last words of the unhappy Victor Frankenstein

POINTS
FOR
UNDERSTANDING

Points for Understanding

1

1 Where was Victor Frankenstein born? In what year?
2 How old was Victor Frankenstein when his younger brother, William, was born?
3 Who was Elizabeth?
4 Why did Frankenstein want to learn more about human life?
5 What did Frankenstein's mother hope that Frankenstein and Elizabeth would do one day?
6 Why is Frankenstein glad that his mother is dead?
7 Who was Henry Clerval?
8 Where did Frankenstein go to study?

2

1 What did Frankenstein want to learn most of all?
2 Why were people frightened of Frankenstein?
3 One day, there was a storm. What suddenly gave Frankenstein an idea?
4 What kind of man did Frankenstein want to make?
5 Frankenstein joined wires to the head, feet and hands. Where did the wires go to?
6 What happened when the lightning hit the roof?
7 Frankenstein had not made a man. What had he made?

3

1 What had happened to Frankenstein's house and laboratory?
2 What was Henry Clerval going to study at Heidelburg?
3 What did Frankenstein decide to do?
4 What terrible news did Frankenstein receive from Geneva?
5 Frankenstein stayed the night in a small village about half a kilometre from Geneva. What had happened in this village?
6 Who had killed Frankenstein's brother?
7 'I could not tell anyone my terrible secret.' What was Frankenstein's terrible secret?

4

1 'She is guilty. We know she killed William.'
    (a)   Why did people think the young woman had murdered William?
    (b)   Where was she now?
    (c)   What was going to happen to her at ten o'clock?
2 Why did Frankenstein think that he was a murderer?
3 Where did Frankenstein go?
4 What did the Monster ask Frankenstein to do?

5

1 How did the Monster find out that he was so ugly?
2 How had the Monster learned Frankenstein's name?
3 What promise had the Monster made to himself?
4 Why was the old man not afraid of the Monster?
5 What happened when the young people saw the Monster?
6 One day, the Monster met a child.
    (a)   Why did he go to the child?
    (b)   Why did he kill the child?
    (c)   Why did he put the picture in the young woman's hands?

6

1 What did the Monster ask Frankenstein to create?
2 Why had the Monster brought unhappiness to the world?
3 Where must the Monster live if Frankenstein agreed to his request?
4 What did Frankenstein's father want him to do?
5 Frankenstein asked Elizabeth to wait for him. What was her reply?
6 Why did Frankenstein decide to go to Strasbourg?
7 What did Frankenstein plan to do when he got to Strasbourg?

7

1 What did Frankenstein start doing in Strasbourg?
2 One night, Frankenstein forgot to lock the door of his laboratory. What happened?
3 What did Henry Clerval think might happen if the Monsters had children?
4 What did Henry begin to do?
5 How did Henry Clerval die?
6 What happened to Frankenstein?

8

1 What did Frankenstein say when he was ill?
2 Frankenstein's father said that Frankenstein did not kill William or Henry Clerval. Why was it not possible?
3 Why did Frankenstein always carry a gun with him?
4 Where did Frankenstein and Elizabeth stay on their wedding night?
5 Why did Frankenstein leave Elizabeth alone in the room?
6 What was the Monster's revenge?

9

1 'Now the journey is ended,' said Frankenstein.
    (a) What is the place where the journey ends like?
    (b) Why does Frankenstein think he will be able to kill the Monster?
2 'You are guilty, Frankenstein,' the Monster cried.
    (a) Why does the Monster think that Frankenstein is guilty?
    (b) What is Frankenstein's reply to these words of the Monster?
3 How is the Monster going to end his life?
4 What does Frankenstein decide to do?

Exercises

Background
Who wrote this story?
Mary Shelley wrote this story in 1818 when she was twenty-one years old. She was the second wife of a famous poet called Percy Shelley. Percy and Mary were good friends with another very famous English poet called Lord Byron. The three friends stayed together in Switzerland in 1818. Mary wrote the story of *Frankenstein* very quickly during their stay.

Who was Frankenstein?
Many people think that Frankenstein is the name of the Monster in the story. In fact it is the name of the Monster's creator. Victor Frankenstein was born in 1810 in the beautiful city of Geneva, in Switzerland. His mother died when he was eighteen and three weeks later he left the city. He went to the great German University of Heidelburg, where he studied science. He wanted to learn everything about the human body.

Answer the questions.

1 Who was Mary Shelley's husband?

....

2 In which year did Mary Shelley write *Frankenstein*?

....

3 Was Mary Shelley writing about the past?

....

4 In which year did Victor Frankenstein go to Heidelburg?

....

5 What did Victor Frankenstein study at Heidelburg?

....

6 Is *Frankenstein* a book of fact or fiction?

....

People in the Story

Write short notes from the box next to the correct picture.

Henry Clerval - studied science at Heidelburg University - born in 1822 - hated the Frankenstein family - William - parents died in 1824 - Victor Frankenstein - wife died in 1828 - born in 1810 - married Victor - The Monster - about ten years old when he was killed - friend of Victor - lived with the Frankenstein family - big and ugly - father of two sons - taught languages in Strasbourg - was not born but was made from body parts - Victor's father - Elizabeth

1   *Elizabeth*

2

3

4

5

6

The Monster's Story

Complete the gaps. Use each word in the box once.

> revenge   understand   face   smiled   hated   saw   through
> know   food   promise   man   never   fear   found   friends
> fruit   water   drink   horrible   eat   skin   name   cloak
> cover   pocket   enemy   time   die   _fire_   away

'I remember the heat of the ¹......_fire_......,' the Monster said. 'I remember
running ²............................ from it. I ran and ran ³...............................
the city. It was dark and no one ⁴...................................... me.
I did not know who I was. I did not ⁵......................................
where I was going. Many days passed.'

'How did you live?' I asked him. 'What did you ⁶...................................?'

'Sometimes I ate ⁷... from the trees,'
the Monster answered. 'Sometimes I took ⁸...............................
from houses. The first ⁹.. I did this, a
¹⁰.................................. saw me. I shall ¹¹..................................... forget
the ¹²............................... in his eyes. I could not ¹³................................
it. I wanted to be ¹⁴...................................... with him. I
¹⁵...................................... at him, but he ran away.

'A few days later, I came to a small pool of ¹⁶.. .
When I bent down to ¹⁷......................................., I saw my own
¹⁸.. . How ¹⁹... it was!
How different from other people's faces! I saw my yellow, wrinkled
²⁰.. . I saw my yellow eyes and thin, black lips.
Now I knew why people ran away from me. From that moment, I
²¹.. myself. And I hated you, Victor Frankenstein.'

'How do you know my ²²...?' I cried.

'The laboratory was on fire,' the Monster replied. 'I picked up your
²³.. to protect myself from the fire. I used it
to ²⁴... myself. Later, I ²⁵...
a book in the ²⁶.. with your
name in it. I made a ²⁷... to myself.
Everyone with that name was my ²⁸.. .
Everyone with that name would ²⁹.. .
I would wander through the world looking for my ³⁰.............................. .'

Comprehension

Answer the questions.

1 What was the Monster running away from?

....

2 What was on fire?

....

3 Why did no one see the Monster?

....

4 Where was the Monster going?

....

5 Where did the Monster find food?

....

6 The first man who saw the Monster ran away. Why did the man
do this?

....

7 Did the monster want to hurt the man?

....

8 Why did the Monster stop at the pool of water?

   ....

9 What did the Monster see when he looked in the pool of water?

   ....

10 Why did the Monster hate Victor Frankenstein?

   ....

11 Where did the Monster find the book with Frankenstein's name
   in it?

   ....

12 What is the meaning of *revenge*?

   ....

Write questions for the answers.

1 *Where did the monster run?*
   The monster ran through the city.

2 *Where* ....
   The Monster went into the mountains.

3 *How* ....
   He stayed in the mountains for many days.

4 *When* ....
   This happened in 1832.

5 *How* ....
   He knew that people were afraid of him because they ran away.

6 *When* ....
   He realised his face was horrible when he looked in a pool of water.

7 *Why* ....
   He hated Frankenstein because he had made him ugly.

8 *What* ....
A cloak is an old-fashioned coat.

9 *Why* ....
The Monster put on the cloak to protect himself from the fire.

10 *What* ....
He found a book in the pocket of the cloak.

11 *Who* ....
Everyone with the Frankenstein name was the Monster's enemy.

12 *What* ....
He wanted to make Victor Frankenstein's life as unhappy as his own.

Making Sentences

Put the words in the correct order to make full sentences.

1 to make Frankenstein a man wanted Victor.
Victor Frankenstein wanted to make a man.
....

2 the good man wanted to be Frankenstein.

....

3 alive The came during a Monster thunderstorm.

....

4 because The Monster was bad everyone became afraid of him.

....

5 see The Monster's man could not face the blind.

....

6 The Monster man's gun fired a blind at the son.

....

7 a wife agreed for Frankenstein to make the Monster.

....

8 far other The Monster to live agreed from people.

....

9 Monster's destroyed the Henry wife..

....

10 many countries across the Monster followed Frankenstein.

....

11 they came to ice and snow At the last of land.

....

12 themselves Monster both Frankenstein the killed and.

....

Frankenstein's Diary

Look at the notes from Frankenstein's diary. Write full sentences.

1 14 Jan: Working v hard. Profs think I'll be famous scientist one day.
   14th January: I'm working very hard. The professors think I will be a
   famous scientist one day.

2 2 March: letter from Elizabeth – wants to visit – but impossible
   – too busy with work

....

....

....

3 16 May: Rd more amazing bks about death in library. Want to
   see dead man.

....

....

....

4   12 July: Spent pm at hospital, talking to old pple, looking at
    their bodies. 2 men died. Rd till 2am.

    ....

    ....

    ....

5   12 Sept: accident today - young man killed - will ask for body

    ....

    ....

    ....

    ....

Writing

Write the people's stories, answering the questions.

1   You are the man the Monster meets the first time he takes food
    from a house.

> What did the Monster look like? What did the Monster do when
> he saw you? What did you do?

I came home, walked into my house and saw a man in my kitchen. When he
....
turned round, I was terrified.
....

....

....

....

....

....

....

....

....

....

....

2 You are the blind man the Monster makes friends with.

> What did the Monster say to you when he came into your house for the first time? What did you talk about when the Monster came to visit? What happened when your daughter came home early one day?

I was at home one day on my own. I heard a knock at the door, and a man

came in.

....

....

....

....

....

....

....

....

....

....

....

Published by Macmillan Heinemann ELT
Between Towns Road, Oxford OX4 3PP
Macmillan Heinemann ELT is an imprint of
Macmillan Publishers Limited
Companies and representatives throughout the world
Heinemann is a registered trademark of Harcourt Education, used under licence.

ISBN 1–405072–67–9
EAN 978–1–405072–67–0

This retold version by Margaret Tarner for Macmillan Readers
First published 1986
Text © Margaret Tarner 1986, 1992, 2002, 2005
Design and illustration © Macmillan Publishers Limited 1998, 2002, 2005

This edition first published 2005

Illustrated by Victor Ambrus
Original cover template design by Jackie Hill
Cover photography by Corbis/Bettmann

Printed in Thailand

2009 2008 2007 2006 2005
10 9 8 7 6 5 4 3 2 1